# Grandmother's Flower Garden

The Classic QUILT Series #2

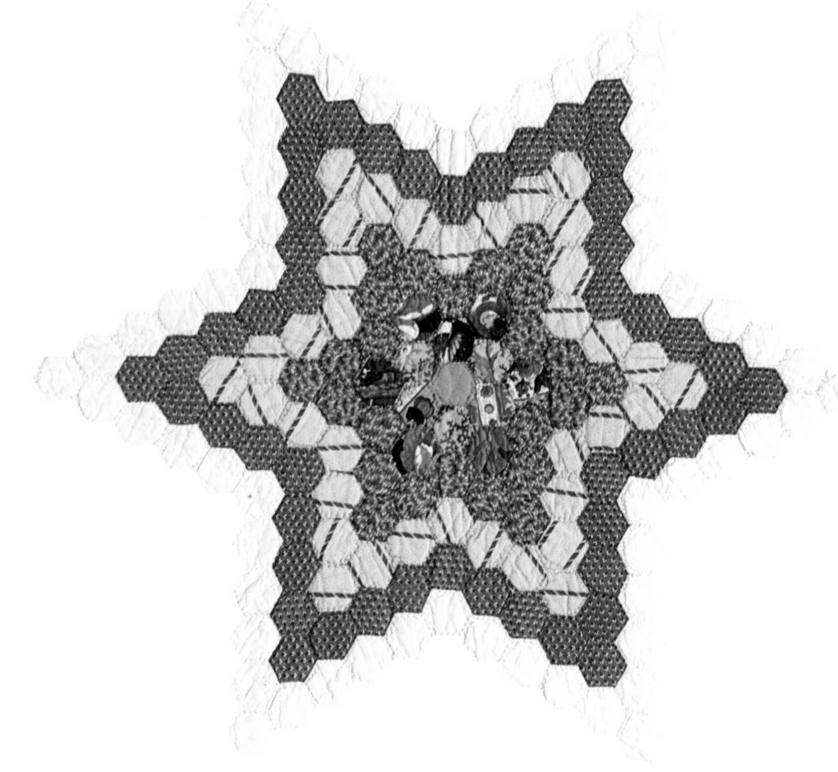

LAURA NOWNES

*The Quilt Digest Press ⁕ San Francisco*

 Published in the United States of America by The Quilt Digest Press, San Francisco.

Editorial and production direction by Michael Kile.
Book editing by Harold Nadel.
Book and cover design by Kajun Graphics.
Quilt photography by Sharon Risedorph and Karen Steffens.
Cover and room setting photographs by Sharon Risedorph.
Computer graphics by Kandy Petersen.
Typographical composition by DC Typography.
Printed by Nissha Printing Company, Ltd., Kyoto, Japan.
Color separations by the printer.
Home graciously lent by Michael and Marion Gates.

*For two special grandmothers, Jane and Naomi.*

First Printing.

Library of Congress Cataloging-in-Publication Data

Nownes, Laura, 1953-
Grandmother's flower garden / Laura Nownes.
p. cm.
ISBN 0-913327-22-0 (pbk.) : $6.95
1. Quilting–Patterns. 2. Flowers in art. I. Title.
TT835.N684 1990
746.9'7–dc20 90-42336
CIP

The Quilt Digest Press
955 Fourteenth Street
San Francisco 94114

# INTRODUCTION

*Grandmother's Flower Garden:* just the name creates a warm feeling of coziness and familiarity. It reminds us of a more gentle and relaxed way of life when grandmothers baked bread, tended their gardens and still had time to make handsewn quilts.

This classic quilt pattern requires you to slow down and enter the world of hand sewing. This is not a make-it-in-a-day quilt, but a family heirloom to be treasured for years to come. If you are like many quiltmakers, you may have several projects going at once. *Grandmother's Flower Garden* is a good one to return to between others. The fabric and paper guides used to make your quilt can be tucked into a handbag or suitcase for lunchtime sewing, sewing while waiting for an appointment or travel stitching.

Here are three *Grandmother's Flower Garden* quilts to stimulate your creativity. They are as different from each other as any three quilts of the same pattern can be. With such variety, you can choose which one you want to make *first.* Each comes with:

- A full-color photograph of the quilt
- A bed and wall-size chart, if appropriate
- A yardage chart
- Cutting and sewing instructions
- Accurate templates

Once you've made one, you'll probably want to try both of the others. And, once you've made a *Grandmother's Flower Garden* (or three!) from this book, you may decide to design a variation of your own.

Happy quilting!

Laura

Laura Nownes

## HERE'S HOW

Use the helpful chart below which gives mattress sizes and suggested quilt sizes. With the exception of the crib quilt, all suggested quilt sizes allow for a 14″ drop on three sides. It is always advisable to measure your bed or wall space to determine the desired size you would like to make. Then look at the chart accompanying the pattern variation you have chosen and select the quilt size which comes closest to your desired finished size.

| Mattress size | Suggested quilt size |
|---|---|
| Crib: 27″ × 52″ | 45″ × 60″ |
| Twin: 39″ × 75″ | 67″ × 89″ |
| Double: 54″ × 75″ | 82″ × 89″ |
| Queen: 60″ × 80″ | 88″ × 94″ |
| King: 76″ × 80″ | 104″ × 94″ |
| California King: 72″ × 84″ | 100″ × 98″ |

Two simple construction techniques are given below: English piecing and hand piecing. Individual shapes (hexagons) are joined together to form units: for example, rosettes, diamonds or stars. Each pattern requires a lattice of hexagons to separate the units from each other and join them to form a completed quilt top. At first glance, the diagrams may appear strange, and you may find yourself wondering how all this will work. Don't worry: these units (with appropriate lattices) will fit together like a jigsaw puzzle. Carefully study the assembly diagram for the quilt you are working on to make sure your units are correctly positioned before sewing.

Read through both of the techniques and choose the one which feels more comfortable.

## WHAT YOU NEED

Fabric: 100% cotton—see individual quilts for exact amounts
Template plastic
Black ultra-fine permanent pen
Paper scissors
Marking pencil
Glass-head pins
Fabric scissors
Thin, light-colored thread for basting
Needle, #9 or #10 Between
Cotton thread
Small scissors
Small C-Thru (1″ × 6″) ruler *(optional)*
Batting

## ENGLISH PIECING

Like many beginning quilters, my first quilt was a sampler. It included a *Grandmother's Flower Garden* block. This is when I was first introduced to English piecing construction. I was impressed with its simplicity and delighted with the results; every corner matched perfectly. What a satisfying reward for a beginner!

To achieve such accuracy, you need a paper guide for every shape. *The accuracy of the paper guide is important.* To save you time in marking your own guides, we have included a page of hexagons, in each of three sizes, for the three quilts included in this book. You can easily make photocopies of the page needed and then use your paper scissors to cut out the individual shapes. As you will need a guide for each shape, you will want to make several copies.

1. Make a plastic template of the *larger* hexagon (the one which includes seam allowance).
2. Layer your fabric (4 to 6 thicknesses) with the wrong side facing up. Place the template shape onto the fabric and use a marking pencil to trace around the edges. Trace more shapes, filling the piece of fabric. To save fabric, butt the sides of the shapes together so that there is a common line between shapes, similar to our guide pages.
3. Place a pin at the center of each traced shape in order to hold the layers securely.
4. Use your fabric scissors to cut out all of the fabric shapes. You may want to organize and store shapes from the same fabric in small plastic bags to avoid losing them.
5. Make the paper guides. Trace your own, using the *smaller* hexagon shape (the one without seam allowance), or make photocopies of one of our pages and cut them apart.
6. Center a paper guide on the wrong side of a fabric shape. Secure it with a pin.
7. Thread your needle with a single strand of basting thread with a knot at one end. Fold one edge of the seam allowance to the wrong side of the shape. Hold it in place with your free hand. With the knot on the right side, stitch through all thicknesses. Stitch up to the corner, bring the needle and thread to the right side, and make a sharp fold in the fabric at the corner (being careful not to round off the corners). Continue stitching around the shape, making sharp folds at each corner. Finish with a back stitch to secure the thread.

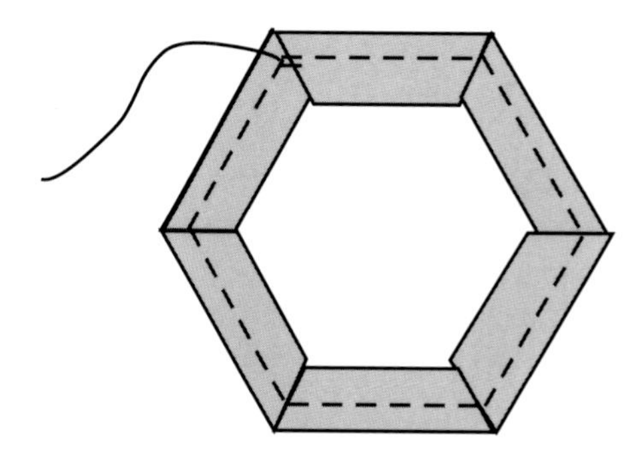

*Step 7*

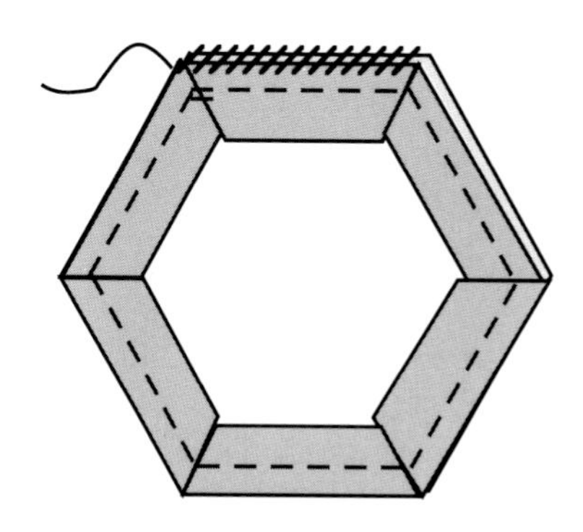

*Step 9*

8. Repeat Steps 6 and 7 for additional fabric shapes. You may want to pre-cut enough fabric shapes and paper guides so that you can construct a complete rosette or star in one sitting.

9. To join shapes, place their right sides together and corners in line with each other. Thread your needle with a single strand of cotton thread with a knot at one end. Use a small whipstitch to join two edges to each other, as shown. Catch only the folded edges of the shapes, trying not to stitch into the paper guide.

10. Using the same technique, join enough shapes to make the desired unit (rosette, diamond, star, etc.).

11. The paper guides on the outer edges of the completed unit need to stay intact until other units (such as lattice) have been joined to them. However, the paper guides for the hexagons within the unit can be removed. Clip and remove the basting threads, and then carefully pull out the paper guides.

12. Join all of the completed units together, referring to the assembly diagrams for the quilt you have chosen. Remove any remaining paper guides.

## HAND PIECING

Hand piecing is another easy method of accurately joining shapes. It differs from English piecing in that a paper guide is not required. The finished size, however, is marked onto the wrong side of each fabric shape as a guide for stitching. Stitches *never* extend into the seam allowance.

1. Make a plastic template of the *larger* hexagon (the one which includes seam allowance).

2. Layer your fabric (4 to 6 thicknesses) with the wrong side facing up. Place the template shape onto the fabric and use a marking pencil to trace around the edges. Trace more shapes, filling the piece of fabric. To save fabric, butt the sides of the shapes together so that there is a common line between shapes, similar to our guide pages.

3. Place a pin at the center of each traced shape to hold the layers securely.

4. Use your fabric scissors to cut out all of the fabric shapes. You may want to organize and store shapes from the same fabric in small plastic bags to avoid losing them.

5. Make a plastic template of the *smaller* hexagon (the one without seam allowance). With the wrong side of a fabric shape up, center the template and use the marking pencil to mark

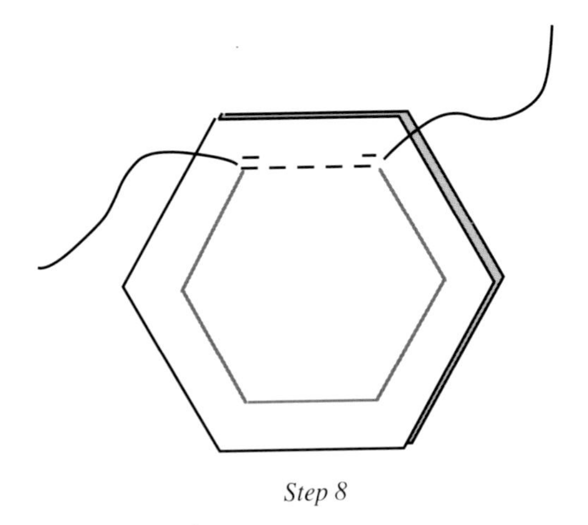

*Step 8*

around the edges. These stitching lines should be 1/4" from the cut edges.

*– OR –*

Use your small C-Thru ruler and marking pencil to mark a line 1/4" in from the cut edges. These are the stitching lines.

6. Thread your needle with a single strand of cotton thread. Do not secure the end with a knot.

7. Place two fabric shapes right sides together, with edges and corners even.

8. Beginning and ending with two small backstitches, join the shapes with small hand running stitches, exactly as shown. Do *not* stitch into the seam allowance. Check often to see that the stitches on the underlying shape continue on the marked stitching line.

9. Additional shapes can be added in the same manner, working around the center shape. To save thread, you need not cut the thread between shapes. Simply bring the needle and thread through the seam allowance to the edges of the new shapes, begin with two small backstitches and continue sewing.

10. Continue adding shapes to form the desired unit (rosette, diamond, star, etc.).

11. Join all of the completed units together, referring to the assembly illustrations for the quilt you have chosen.

# ROSETTES

*Maker unknown, c.1930. Collection of Linda Reuther/Hearts and Hands, San Anselmo, California.*

| ¾″ Hexagon | CRIB | TWIN | DOUBLE/ QUEEN | KING |
|---|---|---|---|---|
| **Finished Size** | 36″ × 47″ | 66″ × 91″ | 81″ × 92″ | 111″ × 101″ |
| **Units set** | 2 × 4 | 4 × 9 | 5 × 9 | 7 × 10 |

| | CRIB | TWIN | DOUBLE/ QUEEN | KING |
|---|---|---|---|---|
| **# Rosettes:** | | | | |
| # Unit A | 8 | 36 | 45 | 70 |
| # Unit B | 3 | 24 | 32 | 54 |
| **# Top and Bottom Units:** | | | | |
| # Unit C | 1 | 3 | 4 | 6 |
| # Unit D | 1 | 3 | 4 | 6 |
| **FABRIC NEEDS (YARDS)** | | | | |
| **Rosette centers** | $\frac{1}{8}$ | $\frac{1}{2}$ | $\frac{1}{2}$ | $\frac{3}{4}$ |
| **First row—solids** | $\frac{1}{4}$ | $1\frac{1}{4}$ | $1\frac{1}{2}$ | $2\frac{1}{2}$ |
| **Second row—prints** | 1 | $3\frac{1}{4}$ | 4 | 6 |
| **Light background** | $1\frac{1}{2}$ | $5\frac{1}{2}$ | $6\frac{1}{2}$ | 9 |
| **Lattice** | 1 | $3\frac{1}{4}$ | 4 | 6 |
| **Backing** | $1\frac{1}{2}$ | $5\frac{3}{8}$ | $5\frac{1}{2}$ | $8\frac{3}{4}$ |
| **CUTTING YOUR FABRIC** | | | | |
| *Use templates C and D.* | | | | |
| **Rosette centers** | 11 | 60 | 77 | 124 |
| **First row—solids** | 70 | 372 | 478 | 768 |
| **Second row and border—prints** | 252 | 988 | 1226 | 1874 |
| **Light background** | 430 | 1600 | 1970 | 2976 |
| **Lattice** | 264 | 1004 | 1244 | 1896 |
| **Backing:** number of lengths | 1 | 2 | 2 | 3 |

## MAKING YOUR QUILT

1. Use either hand piecing or English piecing methods to make the required number of rosettes, as shown.
2. Make the required number of top and bottom units, as shown.
3. Add lattices to the rosettes to make the required number of A and B units. Refer to the illustrations for exact placement of the lattices.
4. Add lattices to the top and bottom units to make the required number of C and D units. Refer to the illustrations for exact placement of the lattices.
5. Refer to the illustration for the exact layout position of the completed units.
6. Join Units A, B, C and D, as shown. Notice that additional lattices are necessary to fill in around the edges.
7. Attach one row of light background shapes all the way around the edge of the quilt top. Next, attach a row of print shapes and then another row of light background shapes around the entire edge of the quilt top, as shown in the photo. Add a final row of lattice.
8. Your quilt top is now ready to be quilted or tied.
9. To finish the edges, cut the backing even with the front. Then, turn the front and backing in $\frac{1}{4}''$ toward each other. Hand stitch together along the outer edge.

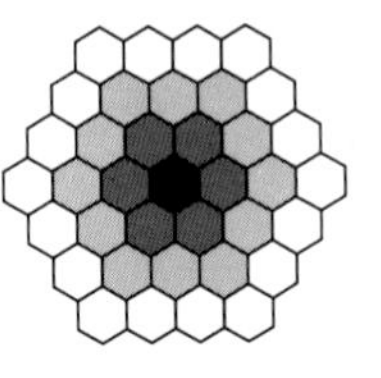

*Rosette*

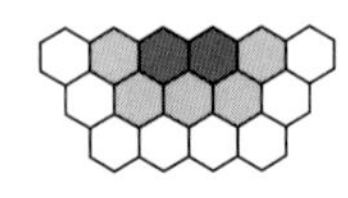

*Top and Bottom Units*

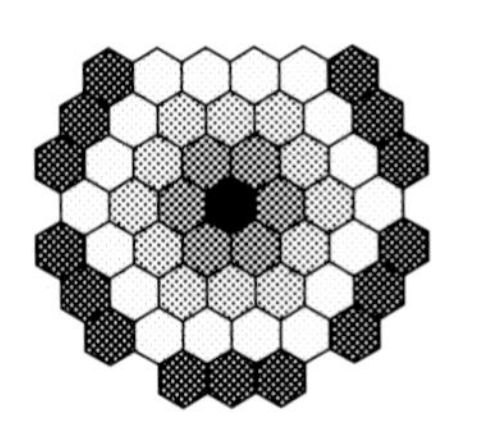

*Unit A*

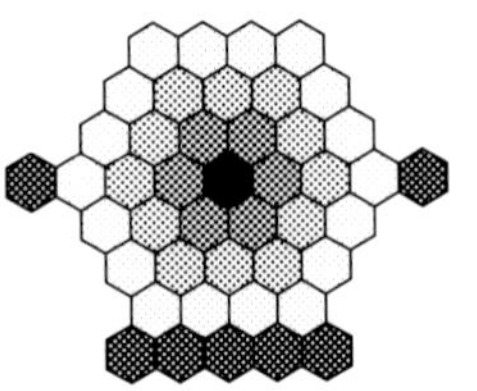

*Unit B*

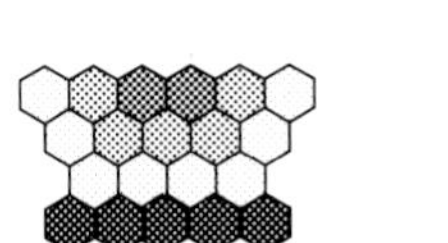

*Unit C*

*Unit D*

*Step 5*

*Step 6*

# STARS AND ROSETTES

*Maker unknown, c.1940. Collection of Robert and Ardis James.*

This is an original setting. Yardage is given for one size only. However, a smaller quilt finishing approximately 63″ × 63″ can be made by using templates C and D (3/4″ hexagon). If you wish to copy the quilt shown, you will notice that the units on the edges have not been cut off symmetrically. Enough yardage is allowed for making complete half units for the corners. You can decide at what point you want to cut them off once they have been joined to other units.

| 1⅛″ Hexagon | King |
|---|---|
| **Finished size** | 97″ × 97″ |
| **# Stars** | 5 |
| **# Half stars** | 2 |
| **# Rosettes** | 8 |
| **# Half rosettes** | 8 |
| **FABRIC NEEDS (YARDS)** | |
| **Light background** | 3½ |
| **Stars:** | |
| Center | ¼ |
| First row | ½ |
| Second row | ½ |
| Third row | 1 |
| Fourth row | 1⅜ |
| **Rosettes:** | |
| Center | ¼ |
| First row | ½ |
| Second row | ¾ |
| Third row | 1 |
| Fourth row | 1⅜ |
| **Lattice** | 2¾ |
| **Borders and binding** | 2¾ |
| **Backing** | 5½ |
| **CUTTING YOUR FABRIC** | |
| *Use templates E and F.* | |
| **Light background** | 730 |
| **Stars:** | |
| Center | 7 |
| First row | 74 |
| Second row | 146 |
| Third row | 218 |
| Fourth row | 290 |
| **Rosettes:** | |
| Center | 16 |
| First row | 80 |
| Second row | 152 |
| Third row | 224 |
| Fourth row | 296 |
| **Lattice** | 430 |
| **Backing:** number of lengths | 2 |
| **Borders** | Two at 4¾″ × 98″ |

## MAKING YOUR QUILT

1. Use either hand piecing or English piecing methods to make 5 stars, as shown.
2. Make 2 half stars, as shown.
3. Make 8 rosettes, as shown.
4. Make 8 half rosettes, as shown.
5. Add lattices to each star and each half star. Refer to the illustrations for exact placement of the lattices.
6. The position of the lattices on the rosettes is not the same on each unit. Refer to the assembly illustration for the exact placement.
7. Join the units together, referring to the assembly illustration for exact placement of each unit.
8. Attach border strips to two opposite sides of the quilt top, as shown in the photo. Trim off any excess length.
9. Your quilt top is ready to be quilted or tied.

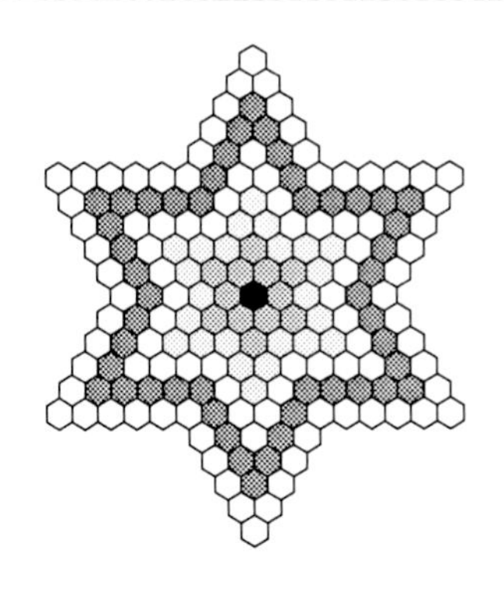

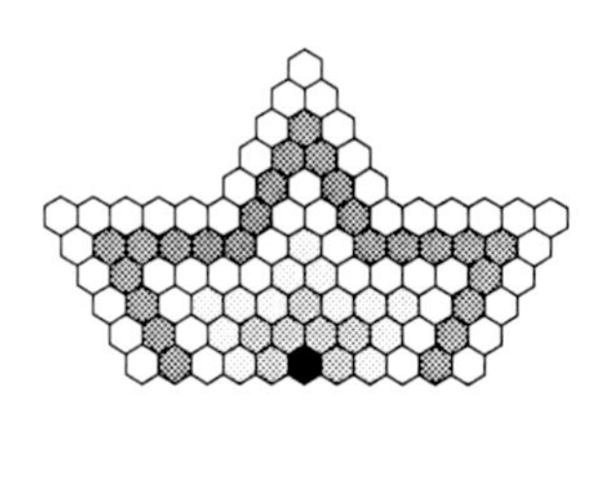

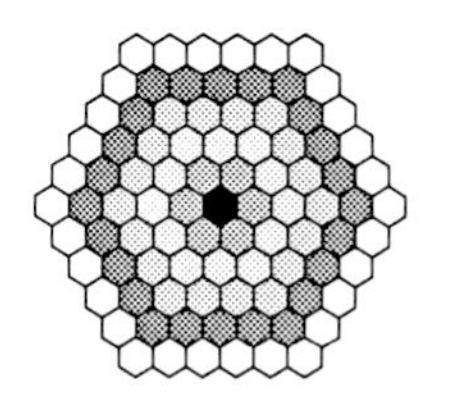

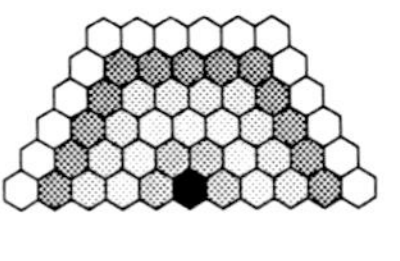

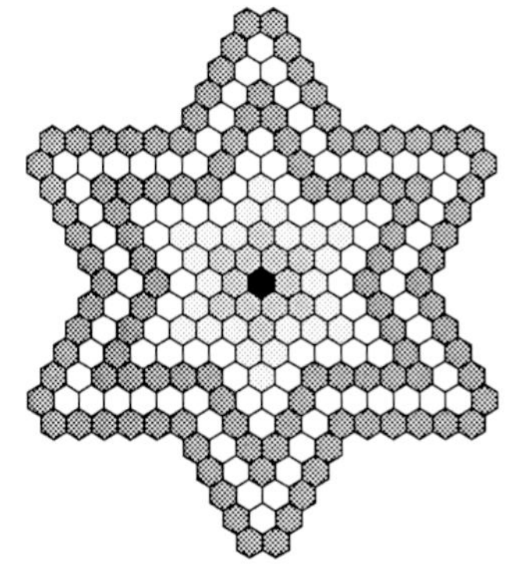

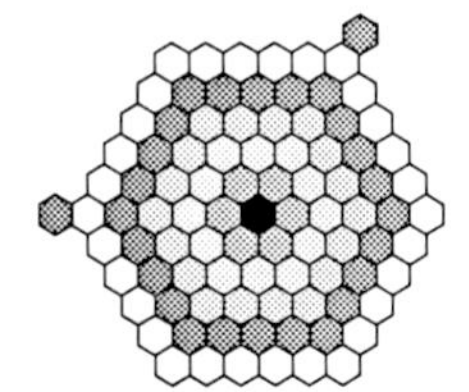

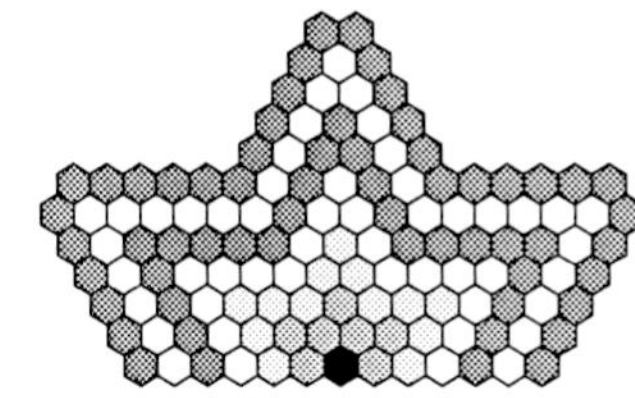

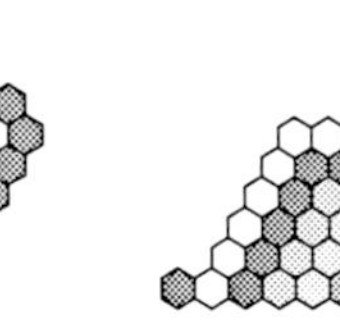

*Step 5*

*Step 5*

*Steps 6-7*

# DIAMONDS

*Maker unknown, c.1860. Collection of Robert and Ardis James.*

| ⅝″ Hexagon | Twin | King |
|---|---|---|
| **Finished size** | 58″ × 72″ | 90″ × 104″ |
| **# Diamonds** | 36 | 90 |
| **# Side Units** | 12 | 24 |
| **# Corner Units** | 6 | 6 |

## FABRIC NEEDS (YARDS)

| | | |
|---|---|---|
| **Diamond centers and binding** | 5/8 | 1 |
| **First row—solids** | 3/4 | 1 3/8 |
| **Second row—prints** | 1 3/8 | 2 1/2 |
| **Muslin row** | 1 3/4 | 4 |
| **Lattice**, side and corner units | 1 3/4 | 4 |
| **Backing** | 4 1/2 | 9 |

## CUTTING YOUR FABRIC

*Use templates A and B.*

| | | |
|---|---|---|
| **Diamond centers** | 55 | 121 |
| **First row—solids** | 288 | 720 |
| **Second row—prints** | 576 | 1440 |
| **Muslin row** | 864 | 2160 |
| **Lattice**, side and corner units | 816 | 1782 |
| **Backing:** number of lengths | 2 | 3 |

## MAKING YOUR QUILT

1. Use either hand piecing or English piecing to make the required number of diamonds, as shown.
2. Make the required number of side units, as shown.
3. Make 6 corner units, as shown.
4. Add lattices to each diamond, referring to the illustration for exact placement.
5. Join the units together to make one-sixth of the quilt top, referring to the assembly illustration.
6. Make five more sections, exactly as you did in Step 5.
7. Join sections in pairs. Then attach a corner unit.
8. Join the remaining sections together to complete the quilt top, having a diamond center shape at the centerpoint of the quilt top.
9. Your quilt top is now ready to be quilted or tied.
10. Straighten the edges of the quilt. Then, finish with a 1/4″ binding.

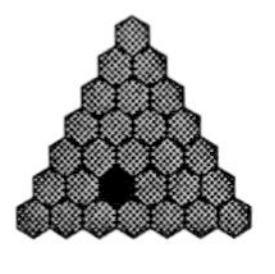

*Side Unit*

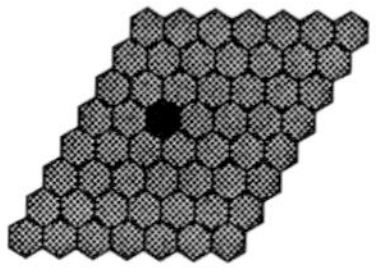

*Corner Unit*

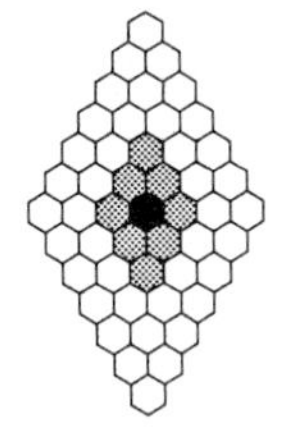

*Step 4*

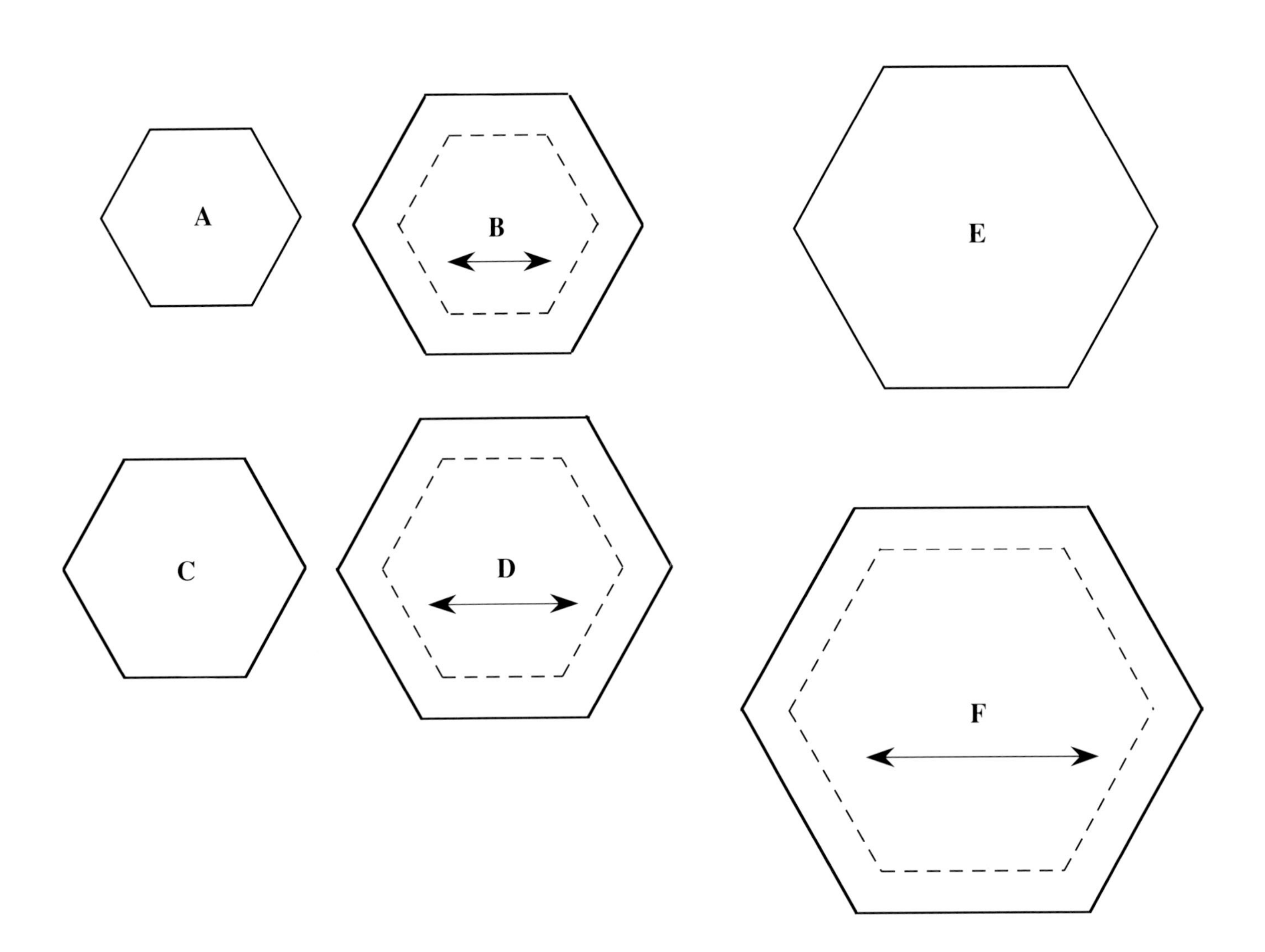

A
B
E
C
D
F

# ⅝″ Hexagon

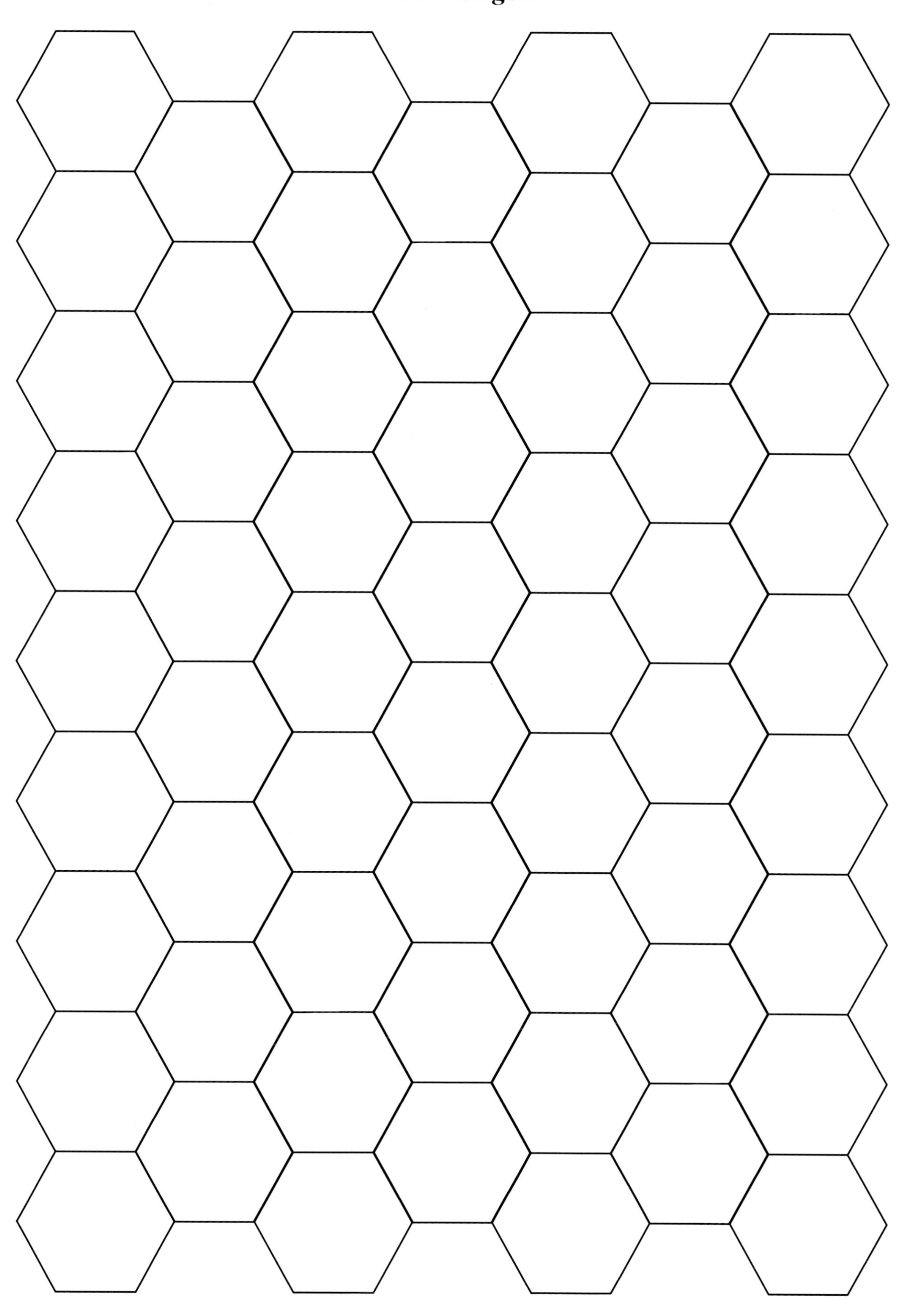

# ¾″ Hexagon

# 1⅛″ Hexagon

THE ART QUILT
HEARTS AND HANDS
The Influence of Women & Quilts on American Society
COLOR AND CLOTH
THE QUILTMAKER'S ULTIMATE WORKBOOK BY MARY COYNE PENDERS
Sunbonnet Sue Makes Her First Quilt
Sunbonnet Sue Goes to the Quilt Show
To Love & To Cherish
Remember Me
QUILTS! QUILTS!! QUILTS!!!
The Complete Guide To Quiltmaking
Quilts Galore!
QUILTMAKING STYLES AND TECHNIQUES
Star of Bethlehem
Double Wedding Ring
Grandmother's Flower Garden
Log Cabin
LAURA NOWNES